LISTEN TO THE LANDSCAPE

Haiku by

Linda Nemec Foster

Hand-colored photographs by

Dianne Carroll Burdick

WILLIAM B. EERDMANS PUBLISHING COMPANY

GRAND RAPIDS, MICHIGAN / CAMBRIDGE, U.K.

Published 2006 by
Wm. B. Eerdmans Publishing Co.
2140 Oak Industrial Drive N.E., Grand Rapids, Michigan 49505 /
P.O. Box 163, Cambridge CB3 9PU U.K.

Printed in the United States of America

10 09 08 07 06   7 6 5 4 3 2 1

ISBN-10: 0-8028-2898-1 / ISBN-13: 978-0-8028-2898-9

www.eerdmans.com

To my mother, Shirley Anne Schemanske Carroll,
and to the memory of my father, Bruce Kenneth Carroll Sr.

— DCB

To Deborah Nemec and Therese Becker,
sister, friend, lovers of the good earth.

— LNF

CONTENTS

A NOTE ON THE IMAGES

One of the keys to haiku poetry is that the first impression of the poet is very important. Poets take a subject from their daily life and add local color to create freshness.

This rings true when looking at Dianne Carroll Burdick's images. She photographs what is around her in her everyday life: a walkway to the beach, a group of trees, an old house by the side of the road. However, she takes these images out of the realm of reality and transforms them into memory. By hand painting black and white photographs, Dianne Carroll Burdick has taken us a step away from a literal meaning and into our own mind's eye.

JILL ENFIELD
author of *Photo-Imaging: A Complete Guide to Alternative Processes*

A NOTE ON THE HAIKU

Land and water play a substantial role in this book. Linda Nemec Foster uses these landscapes as if they were her extended mother. She acutely observes "How the end of the ocean/Becomes land" — the doubleness of knowing how to look inward, back toward the terrain, after so completely looking outward, over the water. For her, the view represents return, not escape or disappearance. Land and water mysteriously become the same medium.

Quintessential to these poems is their sense of acceptance, coming from identification with the landscape. These are poems to read both when you yourself have accepted the inevitable and when you are grappling and fearful of it.

In the spirit of Asian poetry, where the insentient natural world is used to represent the depth of emotional landscape and engagement, Linda Nemec Foster's haiku display her emotional nativity. In this respect, she suggests how wind and dunes, trees and water shape a person's tranquility and contain its turmoil.

DIANE WAKOSKI
author of *The Butcher's Apron* and *Emerald Ice*

ACKNOWLEDGMENTS

For encouragement and direction, my thanks to John M. Carney, professor of art in photography at Western Michigan University in Kalamazoo. For instruction on color theory, my thanks to Richard Stien. For making it all happen, I thank Sandra DeGroot and Eerdmans Publishing for supporting our vision. For digital imaging, promotional materials, advice, support, and patience, my deepest appreciation goes to my husband, Rob Burdick.

DIANNE CARROLL BURDICK

My special thanks to Sandra DeGroot, the project director for this book at Eerdmans Publishing, for her patience, guidance, and understanding; and to my husband, Tony Foster, whose amazing love supports every word I write, every image I envision.

LINDA NEMEC FOSTER

LISTEN TO THE LANDSCAPE

ANOTHER MYSTERY

Dawn or dusk, almost
The same. Each day's birth and death
Edged with gold, calm blue

DIVINING ROD

Between ocean and
Forest, between land and sky,
I point the way home

New Language

Define bare trees — faith,
And the smallest of leaves — hope,
Whisper of wind — love

THREE WORLDS

Dark brown earth, our home
Cobalt blue sea, our journey
Gauze clouds, our longing

HILL KISSING THE OCEAN

Close your eyes, deep friend,
Feel my lips of grass brush past
All fear of water

SEPARATION

On the left, mere dreams
Blue-white sea murmuring waves
On the right, just us

THE FENCE

Necklace of landscape
Charting your destination
Home beyond earth, sky

The Secret

Hushed words bend with dawn
Away from the wildflowers'
Gossip. Clouds hear songs

NEW WORLD

You see the new world
How the end of the ocean
Becomes land, pure flight

DANCE

Shadows dance with sun
Outstretched arms that touch light once
And then, hold the air

FAMILY TREES

Trees wait in silence
Like loved relatives we've lost
Rare leaves we can't find

THE WISDOM OF WILDFLOWERS

Always thrive where least

Expected: above the sea

Small lives on the edge

THE DREAM OF TREES

To walk like the scarves
Of clouds, to abandon land
And never return

ELECTRIC SKY

You cannot turn off
This light. Streams of blue, yellow
Monet's sky plugged in

Cloud's Edge

Like waves in the sky
Clouds mirror the hushed landscape
Sky's edge, water's shore

PLAYGROUND

She wants to run, twirl
Follow the path all the way
To her past: those trees

MYSTERY

East/west, north/south don't
Matter. Could be sage, wild rose
Or what the heart sees

FRIENDSHIP

Hidden where we know
It's waiting — overgrown path,
Cool dusk, small birdsong

GUARDIAN

I rise from earth, I
Shelter all things you give me,
I keep the secrets

HARVEST

The blue becomes mauve
Becomes purple then lush green
Waiting for your hands

WHERE SUNLIGHT SLEEPS

Not in sapphire seas
Or emerald earth, but dark
Amber of fall leaves

MEMORY

Collect the songs from
Childhood. Don't forget the words
That turn straw to gold

THREE SISTERS

They don't need music
To dance, only the faintest
Hint of blue to sing

REMEMBRANCE

Small house of blue sky
Comfort each soul and give it
New songs, new silence

STRANDS

Gilded strands of light
That caress the sky's neckline —
Pale, luminous skin

THE ROAD TO THE FATHER'S HOUSE

It weaves its way through
Your life. The quiet path filled
With trees and shadows

SHADOWS OF TREES

Their thin shadows spread
So delicately, as if
The ground turns to lace

Open Field

Nothing to hold us

Back — except ourselves. Embrace

That green wall of trees

A NOTE ON THE HAND-COLORING PROCESS

I photographed all the images with Kodak 35mm black & white film using Nikon lenses on Nikon N90S cameras. I then printed the images on Kodak Professional Ektalure G Lustre fiber-base black & white paper, a cream-white fine-grain double weight luster paper that is no longer made. When the prints were dry, I treated the paper with an oil-base solvent and colored the images with Marshall and Prismacolor colored pencils.

DIANNE CARROLL BURDICK